DISASTER ZONE
DUST STORMS

by Vanessa Black

pogo

Ideas for Parents and Teachers

Pogo Books let children practice reading informational text while introducing them to nonfiction features such as headings, labels, sidebars, maps, and diagrams, as well as a table of contents, glossary, and index.

Carefully leveled text with a strong photo match offers early fluent readers the support they need to succeed.

Before Reading

- "Walk" through the book and point out the various nonfiction features. Ask the student what purpose each feature serves.
- Look at the glossary together. Read and discuss the words.

Read the Book

- Have the child read the book independently.
- Invite him or her to list questions that arise from reading.

After Reading

- Discuss the child's questions. Talk about how he or she might find answers to those questions.
- Prompt the child to think more. Ask: Have you ever been in a dust storm? Were you prepared?

Pogo Books are published by Jump!
5357 Penn Avenue South
Minneapolis, MN 55419
www.jumplibrary.com

Library of Congress Cataloging-in-Publication Data

Names: Black, Vanessa, author.
Title: Dust storms: disaster zone / by Vanessa Black.
Description: Minneapolis, MN: Jump! Inc. [2017]
Series: Disaster zone
Audience: Ages 7-10. | Includes bibliographical references and index.
Identifiers: LCCN 2016005565 (print)
LCCN 2016006049 (ebook)
ISBN 9781620313978 (hardcover: alk. paper)
ISBN 9781624964442 (ebook)
Subjects: LCSH: Dust storms–Juvenile literature.
Classification: LCC QC958 .B53 2017 (print)
LCC QC958 (ebook) | DDC 551.55/9–dc23
LC record available at http://lccn.loc.gov/2016005565

Series Editor: Jenny Fretland VanVoorst
Series Designer: Anna Peterson
Photo Researcher: Anna Peterson

Photo Credits: Alamy, 20-21; Corbis, 1, 3, 4-5, 13; Getty, 6-7, 10-11, 16-17; iStock, 14-15, 18; Shutterstock, cover, 8-9, 12, 23; Thinkstock, 19.

Printed in the United States of America at Corporate Graphics in North Mankato, Minnesota.

TABLE OF CONTENTS

CHAPTER 1

IT'S A DUST STORM!

You are driving with your dad down an Arizona **highway**. Suddenly the skies darken. You are surrounded by dust.

You hear sand hit the car. You cannot see anything. It's a dust storm!

Your dad pulls over.
He turns off the lights.
You wait. In about
10 minutes, the wall
of dust has passed.

What just happened?

DID YOU KNOW?

Household dust is made up of gross things from around your house, like the crushed bodies of bugs and dead skin cells. But dust storms outdoors are blowing sand. They are also called sand storms.

Strong winds picked up dust and sand from the ground. They swirled together and made a big dust cloud called a **haboob**. It blew to you. Then it blew away.

TAKE A LOOK!

A haboob forms when cold air rushes down from a thunderstorm. The air kicks up material from the ground to create a wall of dust. The wall travels in front of the storm.

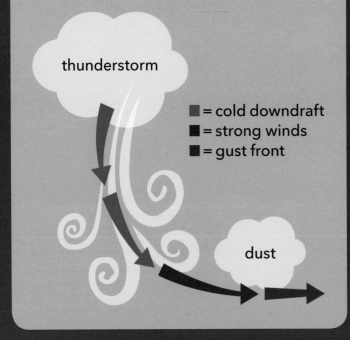

thunderstorm

■ = cold downdraft
■ = strong winds
■ = gust front

dust

haboob · · · ▶

Some dust storms create dust walls over 10,000 feet (3,050 meters) tall. That's taller than some mountains!

Dust storms can carry sand hundreds of miles. They can even travel over the ocean!

WHERE DO THEY HAPPEN?

Most dust storms happen in deserts. But they can happen anywhere there is dry, loose sand.

☐ = Dust Storm-Prone Areas

CHAPTER 2
DEADLY STORMS

It is hard to see in a dust storm. Dust storm accidents kill people every year.

Breathing dust and sand is bad for your lungs. It can give you **asthma** or **lung disease**.

In 2015, dust storms hit the **Middle East**. The wind picked up tons of sand and dust. It blew across countries. For days, people could not see. They had problems breathing. Many people died.

DID YOU KNOW?

Dust storms don't just blow sand around. High winds pick up many things, including clay and soil.

During the 1930s, Americans faced bad dust storms. Farmland was dry. High winds picked up the dry soil and dust. The dust clouds blew across the country. Nothing grew. Cattle died from choking on the dust. People could not make a living.

DID YOU KNOW?

During the Black Blizzard of 1934, black soil from the Great Plains blew east across the country. Twelve million pounds (5.4 million kilograms) of soil fell on Chicago leaving black "snowdrifts."

CHAPTER 3

STAYING SAFE

Meteorologists work hard. They try to warn people about dust storms.

meteorologist · · · · · ▶

They use **satellite images**.
They look at wind **forecasts**.
If they think a dust storm is
likely, they will issue a warning.

Sometimes dust storms come without warning. If you are outside, go inside.

If you plan to be hiking in a desert and cannot get inside, carry a **dust mask** with you. Make sure your eyes, nose, and mouth are covered.

If you have pets, make sure they are inside. If you are on the road, make sure the driver pulls off the road.

Be prepared, and you can stay safe in a dust storm.

ACTIVITIES & TOOLS

MAKE A SAND STORM

What You Need:
- a dust mask
- goggles
- a hairdryer
- fine sand
- potting soil
- a cardboard box larger than a shoe box
- toy cars

1. Bring your supplies outside, or to an area that can get dirty.
2. Put the soil in the bottom of the box.
3. Make a road in the dirt.
4. Put the cars on the road.
5. Put sand over the soil on all parts except the road.
6. Put on the dust mask and goggles. This will protect your eyes, nose, and mouth.
7. Have a parent plug in a hairdryer.
8. Blow the sand with the hairdryer.
9. You've made a sand storm!

asthma: A sickness that causes a person's airways to swell, making it hard to breathe.

dust mask: A covering to protect your nose and mouth.

forecast: An educated guess about what the weather will do.

haboob: A wall of blowing sand or dust.

highway: A major road.

lung disease: Any disease that prevents the lungs from working the way they should.

meteorologist: A person who studies the weather and climate.

Middle East: A region of the world where Africa, Asia, and Europe meet; this region has dry deserts.

satellite images: Pictures taken from space.

INDEX

TO LEARN MORE

Learning more is as easy as 1, 2, 3.

1) Go to www.factsurfer.com

2) Enter "duststorms" into the search box.

3) Click the "Surf" button to see a list of websites.

With factsurfer, finding more information is just a click away.